ABOUT THE PUBLISHER

Microcosm Publishing is Portland's most diversified publishing house and distributor, with a focus on the colorful, authentic, and empowering. Our books and zines have put your power in your hands since 1996, equipping readers to make positive changes in their lives and in the world around them. Microcosm emphasizes skill-building, showing hidden histories, and fostering creativity through challenging conventional publishing wisdom with books and bookettes about DIY skills, food, bicycling, gender, self-care, and social justice. What was once a distro and record label started by Joe Biel in a drafty bedroom was determined to be *Publishers Weekly*'s fastest-growing publisher of 2022 and #3 in 2023, and is now among the oldest independent publishing houses in Portland, OR, and Cleveland, OH. We are a politically moderate, centrist publisher in a world that has inched to the right for the past 80 years.

CONTENTS

UNFUCK YOUR COMMUNICATION WORKBOOK

CONNECT, COLLABORATE, AND MAKE YOURSELF HEARD

Dr. Faith G. Harper, ACS, ACN

Microcosm Publishing
Portland, Ore | Cleveland, Ohio

UNFUCK YOUR COMMUNICATION WORKBOOK:
Connect, Collaborate, and Make Yourself Heard

First edition, July 2025

ISBN 9781648413674

This is Microcosm #900

Cover and book design by Joe Biel

Edited by Kandi Zeller

These worksheets can be used on their own or as a companion to *Unfuck Your Communication.*

Versions of some of the exercises in this book previously appeared in the *Unfuck Your Anger Workbook, Unfuck Your Intimacy, Unfuck Your Boundaries Workbook*, and *Unfuck Your Year.*

For a catalog, write or visit:
Microcosm Publishing
2752 N Williams Ave
Portland, OR 97227

(503) 799 - 2698

All the news that's fit to print at www.Microcosm.Pub/Newsletter

Find more Dr. Faith titles at www.Microcosm.Pub/DrFaith

Get more copies of the book at www.Microcosm.Pub/CommunicationWorkbook

Did you know that you can buy our books directly from us at sliding scale rates? Support a small, independent publisher and pay less than Amazon's price at www.Microcosm.Pub.

To join the ranks of high-class stores that feature Microcosm titles, talk to your local rep: In the U.S. **COMO** (Atlantic), **ABRAHAM** (Midwest), **BOB BARNETT** (Texas, Oklahoma, Arkansas, Lousiana), **IMPRINT** (Pacific), **TURNAROUND** (Europe), **UTP/MANDA** (Canada), **NEW SOUTH** (Australia/New Zealand), **OBSERVATOIRE** (Africa, Europe), **IPR** (Middle East), **YVONNE CHAU** (Southeast Asia), **HARPERCOLLINS** (India), **EVERST/B.K. AGENCY** (China), **TIM BURLAND** (Japan/Korea), and **FAIRE** in the gift trade.

EU Safety Information: https://microcosmpublishing.com/gpsr

Global labor conditions are bad, and our roots in industrial Cleveland in the '70s and '80s made us appreciate the need to treat workers right. Therefore, our books are MADE IN THE USA.

Introduction

Communication. Just the imparting or sharing of information, right? Should be easy. And yet forever getting fucked up. Whether you're communicating at work, school, home, or any other life location, sometimes communicating is challenging, to say the least. And life is hard enough, isn't it? So how might we be able to help? This workbook is full of exercises, activities, and more to help you say what you want to say—to make yourself heard in a world that can be pretty loud.

First, we'll cover what makes up our communication. Then, we'll look at some basic strategies for unfucking everyday communication. After that, we'll discuss specific situations where communication can get really fucked and how to work through those times with practical exercises. Think everything from boundaries to apologies, consent to politics, religion to mental health, etc. And we'll have a whole section of pages devoted to handling and communicating through conflict situations.

You've got this, so let's get talking, writing, and thinking about communicating. But let's start with a grounding exercise.

GROUNDING EXERCISE: THE REORIENTATION COUNTDOWN

Ok, you caught us. This isn't a communication skill. But oftentimes, working through issues that impact our emotional health can be activating. Since communication touches on every aspect of our lives, the thought of working on our skills in that area can be super overwhelming. Memories and current struggles may come up as you work through this book, so we'll begin with a grounding exercise you can come back to at any time if going through this workbook brings up any issues that are emotionally expensive for you.

When we get activated, we get immersed in the situation we are thinking about, past or present, rather than aware of our immediate surroundings. This grounding skill is designed to bring your focus back to the present (reorienting you to the world around you, instead of what your brain started focusing on internally). It's super simple, but what makes it work is you have to look outward instead of inward and it helps you remember your life in the present. It's also referred to as the 5-4-3-2-1 sense game. Because what you are going to do is:

5 things you can see

4 things you can hear

3 things you can smell

2 things you can touch

1 thing you can taste

By focusing on your immediate and present circumstances, it becomes easier to keep yourself in your thinking brain, with all the accompanying executive function skills we like to keep on hand. This will put you in a good frame of mind as you work on practicing and using the communication skills we'll cover in this workbook.

GROUNDING STATEMENT

Part of how the brain thinks it is keeping us safe is to tell us a story about the past, layering it onto the present so we perceive ourselves as reliving a traumatic situation. It's a great safety mechanism in actual dangerous situations . . . but it does nothing to help us deal with and communicate around past issues so we can heal and move forward.

This is a simple exercise for when our brain does this. I encourage everyone to create a grounding statement that reminds them that they are in the present and doing important work.

Stuff like:

This is only a memory. Memories suck, but they can't hurt me.

OR

In the past, I was a victim. Now, I am a survivor.

Come up with one that works for you, make a note of it below and use the shit out of it as needed.

Notes

COMMUNICATION INVENTORY

All of us have different experiences with communication. Reflecting on where you started and where you are with communication can serve as a great foundation for unfucking what you want to say. Use the following prompts to take inventory of your communication history.

What messages did you get about it growing up, in past workplaces and relationships, etc.?

Where do you get into trouble with communication (e.g., saying too much or too little, not being heard, misspeaking, getting distracted, etc.)?

What lessons do you want to unlearn?

What's your history with formal vs. informal communication?

Were you taught to be direct or indirect? What happened when you were too direct or too indirect?

In what areas of your life and/or with what people do communication problems happen?

In what areas and/or with what people do you feel like communication is good?

SO WHAT'S THE PROBLEM, THEN?

Before we can focus on communication solutions, we usually have to wrestle with the problem itself. We have a language that we use to define all aspects of our lives, and the language we use to define our problems—especially our communication problems—can feel extra-shitty at times. Which can shut us down, effectively making problem definition our number one barrier in achieving new goals.

Define the current problem.

Cool, now highlight or underline any words that cause fear, worry, anger, or resistance from you.

Great. Now define those words. Start with "What do I mean by . . ."

Review those definitions. Are they accurate? Helpful? Are there any words that are more accurate? Do any need to be redefined to be useful to your path to move forward? Check back in with yourself. What emotional responses do you have to those words now?

BEING A BADASS CONVERSATIONALIST

Practicing these conversational skills can be a quick and easy way to up your communication game. Practice paying close attention when people talk, asking open ended questions about what the other person says ("What was [blank] like?"), and giving authentic compliments.

- What are some situations in the coming week in which you can challenge yourself to practice your communication skills?
- What are some things you can start a conversation about?
- What are your strengths with communicating with other people?
- How can you draw on those strengths?

ACTION PLAN:

Place	Topic	Result
Grocery store	*Compliment someone on something they're wearing*	*Told someone I liked their shoes, and they smiled and said thank you. I was nervous but it felt nice to make someone else feel good!*

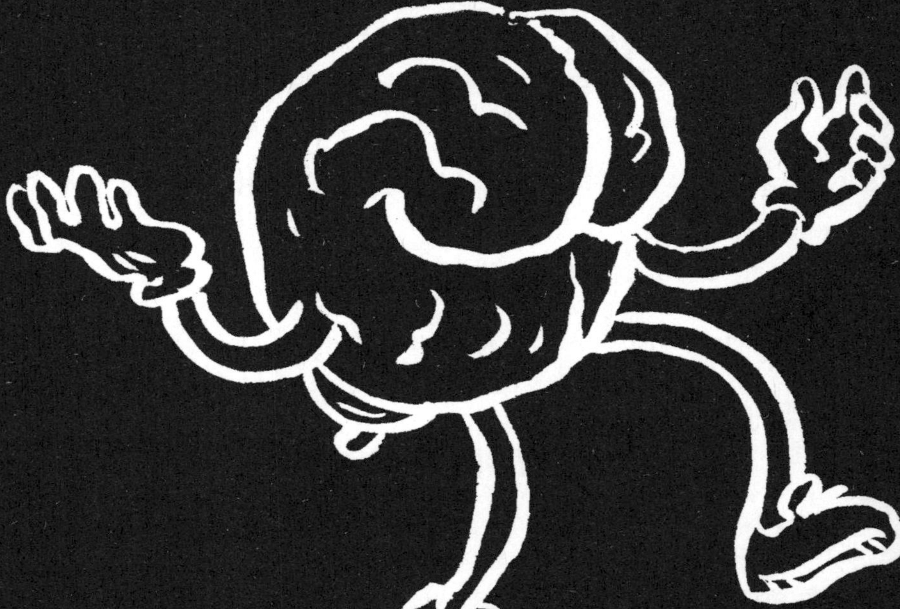

Activities for Identifying Fucked-Up Communication

There are a million ways our communication can get fucked up. The activities in the section take a look at the types, styles, strategies, and levels that make up communication and break them down so you can look at all these angles in your own life, empowering you to say what you want to say. We'll also look at toxic relational patterns in communication to really hone in on specific ways we may be miscommunicating in harmful ways toward ourselves and others.

TYPES OF COMMUNICATION

Generally, the experts divide communication into four different types. However, Dr. Anne Converse Willkomm, a Drexel University professor who teaches a Communications for Professionals course, advocates for five.

Verbal communication is the part most of us think of first. It is the use of our voice to make noises that theoretically convey a shared meaning to the people who hear what we say. It's the words we say and it's how we say them (cadence, pitch, tone, etc.).

What is an example of verbal communication in your life?

Nonverbal communication is the mostly noiseless ways we use our body to share information with others. Our posture. How we use our fingers, hands, and arms to punctuate. Our facial expressions. Our eye contact. Other eye movements (eye rolling, side eye, etc.). Our space between our body and the body of others when we are physically in the same space. Any touch we employ when physically in the same space. We may also make noises that aren't words. Like sighing. Or snapping our tongues on the roofs of our mouths. Or humming. Stuff like that.

What is an example of nonverbal communication in your life?

Written communication is words put somewhere for someone else's eyes to reach them. If you are reading this book on slices of dead tree or on the screen of a device, it's written communication.

What is an example of written communication in your life?

Visual communication is made up of the photos, videos, and other images that share messages. Visual communication may have verbal, nonverbal, and written elements, but it tends to have a more holistic message to share, and often a very emotional one. For example, a photo of a sunset or a video of a kitten making biscuits—things like these share tons of information . . . and can draw us in without any words written or said.

What is an example of visual communication in your life?

And **listening** is the vital fifth type of communication—because every other style relies on it. Receiving what others are sharing and trying to understand what they are working to convey is the entire point of all it. We share information for it to be received. Listening is the act of receiving.

What does listening look like in your life?

STYLES OF COMMUNICATION

Within the above types of communication, we have three communication styles. We can display any of the following styles within any of the types of communication.

An **aggressive** communication style tends to be excessively harsh. Aggressive communicators tend to interrupt others, disregard others' opinions, and continually reinforce their own worldview and "rightness." The meta-message of aggressive communicators is "I'm cool and you're a dumbass."

A **passive** communication style tends to be ineffective in helping people protect themselves and hold their center. Passive communicators often don't make their wants and needs known, and say that things are fine when they are really, totally, deeply not fine. Passive communicators tend to defer to others, praising them while dumping on themselves. *The meta-message of passive communicators is "I'm a hot mess, but you're totally cool, so you make the decisions for both of us."*

An **assertive** communication style is our sweet spot in most cases (unless your literal safety is on the line and being situationally aggressive or passive makes sense). Assertive communicators are firm in their belief systems and speak in a way that is congruent with their actions but still respects differing viewpoints. *The meta-message of assertive communicators is "I'm cool and you're totally cool too. Even if we don't agree."*

Some questions to reflect on:

What is your communication style most of the time? Is it different in different circumstances or with different people?

What messages have you internalized about your right to healthy communication and ownership of your values and beliefs?

If you communicate differently in certain situations, or with certain people, what about those relationships causes you to change?

How close is your current communication style to what your ideal balance would be?

What is the first place you can start to shift your communication style, moving closer to your ideal? How will you go about doing that?

COMMUNICATING WITH PEOPLE WITH DIFFERENT COMMUNICATION STYLES

Later in this book, you're going to see a lot of specific strategies for holding both your ground and your center against weaponized communication. But here is a space for you to recognize different communication styles and build responses that best serve effective communication!

Passive	Aggressive	Assertive
"Whatever you want is fine by me! Oh, Thai food? Sure, it that's what you really want. Oh, no! It's fine by me!"	*"That Thai place you like is gross! I'm not eating that and neither should you!"*	*"You're craving Thai? That place is not my fave, but I know you love it . . . let's pick up Thai food for you, and I can grab a pizza next door. Win-win, baybeeee!"*

STRATEGIES FOR COMMUNICATION

When we face tough communication situations, what strategies do we use? And do they work? Virginia Satir was a therapist and author, and she identified five communication strategies. The first four communication strategies (placating, blaming, computing, distracting) emerge as shields. In other words, we aren't being deliberately shitty, we're being trauma reactive and self-protective . . . even when these strategies no longer serve.

Placaters agree. They tend to do things to please others, to their own detriment. The body posture and voice often demonstrate subservience to the person they are trying to placate. The internet often refers to this as fawning behavior.

When was a time you (or someone you observed) used placating as a strategy? What happened in that situation? Did the communication have the desired effect?

Blamers always disagree as a show of power and autonomy. They may demonstrate intimidating behavior in the process, such as a loud voice or an aggressive stance. Blamers are the most likely to initiate conflict, but that drive generally comes from feeling very alienated.

When was a time you (or someone you observed) used blaming as a strategy? What happened in that situation? Did the communication have the desired effect?

Computers are freakily calm and rational even in heightened emotional conditions. They strive to be ultra-reasonable, which can make them seem unmoving around and dismissive of the feelings of others. A computer is ultra-reasonable, rationalizing and trivializing the content of communication.

When was a time you (or someone you observed) used computing as a strategy? What happened in that situation? Did the communication have the desired effect?

Distractors don't follow the subject at hand at all. They may seem nonsensical, but they are really working to get away from uncomfortable topics by trying to get everyone to pay attention to something safer. If a topic shift doesn't work, they may ignore questions, drift off, act sleepy, etc.

When was a time you (or someone you observed) used distracting as a strategy? What happened in that situation? Did the communication have the desired effect?

Levelers are emotionally balanced. They are assertive about their wants and needs without steamrolling others. This doesn't mean they aren't emotional, but it does mean they're communication is clear regarding their wants and needs and they want problem solving to be beneficial to all parties involved, instead of aiming for some configuration of "you win" or "I win" or "what problem?" Conflict doesn't feel good but it takes less of a toll on their self-worth.

Leveler communication also quickly derails the four more problematic strategies because a leveler uses clear language, coming to their point quickly and redirecting back to it when necessary. They ask others to speak for themselves, request their feedback, acknowledge their experiences . . . all without taking on responsibility for anyone but themselves.

When was a time you (or someone you observed) used leveling as a strategy? What happened in that situation? Did the communication have the desired effect?

LEVELS OF COMMUNICATION

We are all trying to communicate better. But figuring out where the breakdowns come from the most often is also hugely beneficial. I first heard this model in an online course I was streaming on Neuro-Linguistic Programming. I can't find a reference to it anywhere, so I don't know the origin story (and if you do, please drop me a line). Discussing an idea without the appropriate citation and attribution upsets my little academic heart, but it's too brilliant to not share.

The basic idea is that each exchange of verbal dialogue has four levels.

What we mean to say. You know, the actual idea you are trying to express.

What we actually say. If you are really good at saying only exactly what you mean at all times, I hope you write a book on your technique. For us regular humans, what we have in our minds and what comes out of our mouths is not always a solid match.

What the other person hears. Just because you said it doesn't mean they heard it without any filter.

What the other person thinks you mean. Even if you said "anything for dinner is fine" and you meant anything for dinner is fine, your partner may think there is a hidden agenda, or other things going on beyond the words that actually came out of your mouth.

If you got a communication do-over with the above situation, what would you change about the communication on the level(s) where there was a breakdown?

Think about a recent time you experienced a miscommunication. Where in the above levels did things fall apart?

COMMUNICATING WITH PEOPLE AT DIFFERENT LEVELS OF CLOSENESS

There are multiple versions of this level-of-closeness communication model, most of which is based on clinical and philosophical work in the 1960s and 1970s and is often attributed to individuals such as Eric Berne (the psychiatrist responsible for the theory of transactional analysis) and Jesuit philosopher John Powell. But the various versions of this theory are all labeled slightly differently as people have updated language and made the model their own. Below is one such adaptation, and I'm including it here because it is an incredibly helpful tool in determining how our communication shapes our interactions and relationships.

Level 1: Surface-Level Communication

This is just the small-talk, basic exchanges we engage in every day. It can be practical, like telling someone else in line that the next register is open, or apologizing for stepping across someone's line of sight at a concert. It can also mean niceties such as "have a great day" and "thanks, you too" that we share with our barista when we pay for our dirty chai.

The surface-level communication response to "how was your weekend?" might be something like:

"It was good, thank you!"

Level 2: Factual-Level Communication

This level of communication is where we impart information. It's still a very limited exchange, but you are getting a little more than the basic pleasantry.

The factual-level communication response to "how was your weekend?" might be something like:

"Good, but busy! Both of the kiddos had soccer games, so I was running around alot!"

Level 3: Thinking-Level Communication

This level of communication is where we start to show a bit more of who we are, but we are still speaking to opinions or perceptions. Some more risk, but the underlying emotionality is still unsaid.

The thinking-level of communication response to "how was your weekend?" might be something like:

"The kiddos both had soccer games this weekend! I wish the school district hadn't cut their soccer program. I think it's really important for kiddos, and it's been a financial stretch to keep them in sports ever since, but I think it's important to them."

Level 4: Emotional-Level Communication

This level of communication is when we express our emotional lives to someone else. More vulnerability, more asking to be seen and understood. Where our feelings might have been implied in level 3, they are made explicit at this level.

The emotional level of communication response to "how was your weekend?" might be something like:

"I'm tired. The kiddos had soccer games this weekend so I spent the whole time shuttling people in my car and washing uniforms. I really resent the school board for cancelling the soccer program at their school: helping them stay in sports has been a ton of work."

Level 5: Intimate-Level Communication

This level of communication is the level of true intimacy. It is how we share our vulnerability. Our messiness. Our complex humanity with the people who know us and can best support our growth.

The intimate level of communication response to "how was your weekend?" might be something like:

"I am a terrible person. I spent the whole weekend schlepping the kids to soccer games and I just wanted to couch rot while streaming episodes of *Elementary*. And I was the one that signed them up once the soccer program at their school was cancelled. Damn, I'm an asshole for resenting them doing exactly what I expected them to do!"

As we move inward, we are increasing our vulnerability in communication with others. Not everyone is safe or deserving of our innermost essence. My lovely friend Lindo Bacon, in their book *Radical Belonging*, laments that there is no watch that tells you it's time to increase your connection in this manner. Instead, they go on, we are always looking for invitations for further depth from others. But who in our lives invites us to be our full and authentic self?

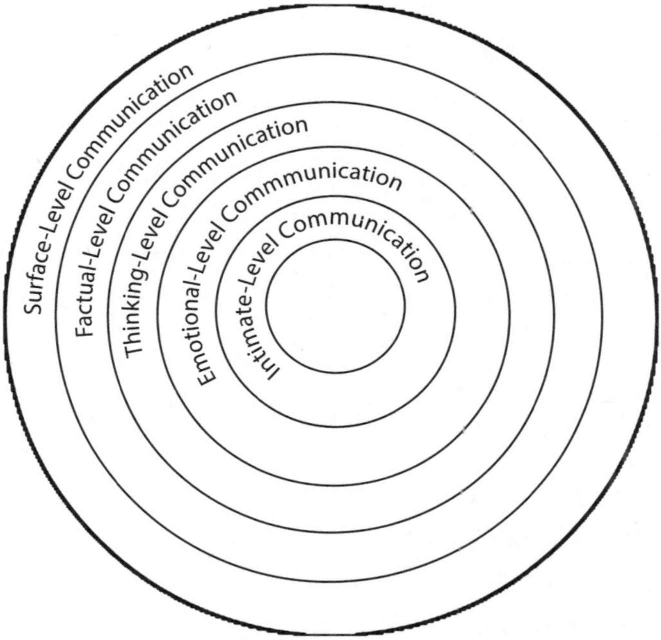

Consider the people in your life that you interact with in some regularity. Write their names in the communication-level circle you currently have them at. Then consider the following questions:

1. How might others communicate with me that they are open to us deepening our connection?
2. How might I communicate that same invitations to others? Which people in the outward circles would I like to focus on?

TOXIC RELATIONAL PATTERNS IN COMMUNICATION

What is a cognitive distortion? A thought we had that we decided to hold on to as a truth . . . even when it's not that true, and not that helpful. It's a story we've become attached to and act from. And it ends up causing problems.

The term "toxic relational strategies" means not just how we think in certain circumstances, but how we interact with others based on those thinking patterns.

These are behaviors everyone is capable of. Everyone has engaged in some of these strategies at some point in their lives. And we have all been victims of these strategies. Not just from perpetrators of abuse, but from otherwise good people who engaged with us in unhealthy ways because they thought that was the best way to meet their needs. The difference is in the degree to which we undertake these strategies.

The purpose of this exercise is to look at patterns of interactions in our own lives, examining the toxic relational strategies that we were subject to as well as ones we have subjected others to. Paying attention to the bidirectional flow of these patterns is the first step in true change.

This list is based on research and training materials from multiple sources including the Safer Society Foundation, the University of Iowa, Moral Reconation Therapy, and my office partner (work wife) Brenda Martinez, who is a trauma-informed licensed professional counselor and licensed sex offender treatment provider. It is not intended to represent the totality of toxic relational patterns, but to start a conversation on how they affect your own life.

Anger as Means of Control: When we use anger to control and manipulate the behavior of others. The difference between this kind of anger and impulsive anger is that the anger response is turned off the minute we get what we want.

Employed by: ◯ Self ◯ Family of Origin ◯ Past Relationships ◯ Current Relationships

Authoritarian Dominance: When we hold rigid boundaries and expectations that things be done "our" way.

Employed by: ◌ Self ◌ Family of Origin ◌ Past Relationships ◌ Current Relationships

Belittling: When we treat others (or their feelings, concerns, point of view) as comparatively unimportant.

Employed by: ◌ Self ◌ Family of Origin ◌ Past Relationships ◌ Current Relationships

Black and White Decreeing: When we term everything in extremes ("I can never trust women" or "All men are players.")

Employed by: ◌ Self ◌ Family of Origin ◌ Past Relationships ◌ Current Relationships

Blaming: When we place blame elsewhere or insist that others are responsible for our behavior. Also could be termed a refusal to accept responsibility.

Employed by: ◌ Self ◌ Family of Origin ◌ Past Relationships ◌ Current Relationships

Compartmentalization of Behavior: When we compartmentalize our behavior to keep from feeling guilty, to justify our actions, or to minimize the seriousness of them. ("I only cheat when out of town for work, never when I'm home.")

Employed by: ◌ Self ◌ Family of Origin ◌ Past Relationships ◌ Current Relationships

Credit Seeking: When we want credit for good behavior ("Okay, I forgot to pay the electric bill and the power was turned off, but don't I get credit for paying the water bill and the Netflix?") or credit for extremes not engaged in ("Okay, I wrecked your car . . . but I could have lied about it and said someone rammed into it while I was at the grocery store") rather than accepting accountability for behavior in question.

Employed by: ◌ Self ◌ Family of Origin ◌ Past Relationships ◌ Current Relationships

Criminal Pride: Feeling a sense of identity and accomplishment from hurting others. ("This is just how I am" or "This is just how I grew up.")

Employed by: ◌ Self ◌ Family of Origin ◌ Past Relationships ◌ Current Relationships

Diverting: When we change the subject to something more comfortable, intentionally redirect the conversation, bring up another problem, or intentionally miss the point of the conversation at hand.

Employed by: ◌ Self ◌ Family of Origin ◌ Past Relationships ◌ Current Relationships

Entitlement: When we think someone owes us something or the world owes us something because we are special, different, or have been through more than others have.
Employed by: ◯ Self ◯ Family of Origin ◯ Past Relationships ◯ Current Relationships

Fact Stacking: When we arrange facts in a way to explain our behavior, while omitting other facts that don't work in our favor.
Employed by: ◯ Self ◯ Family of Origin ◯ Past Relationships ◯ Current Relationships

Fairness Violation: When we believe that everyone is treating us unfairly and/or when we keep a mental scorecard regarding "fairness" in the relationship.
Employed by: ◯ Self ◯ Family of Origin ◯ Past Relationships ◯ Current Relationships

Fight Instigating: When we encourage others to fight, then we stand back and watch.
Employed by: ◯ Self ◯ Family of Origin ◯ Past Relationships ◯ Current Relationships

Frequency Minimization: When we minimize the behavior based on frequency. (It didn't happen five times, it was three times at most!) This is a form of playing defense attorney.
Employed by: ◯ Self ◯ Family of Origin ◯ Past Relationships ◯ Current Relationships

Gaslighting: When we deliberately obscure or twist facts to make others question their reality, memory, and ultimate sanity.
Employed by: ◯ Self ◯ Family of Origin ◯ Past Relationships ◯ Current Relationships

Grandiosity: When we make little things into huge, important things so we can shift the focus of attention.
Employed by: ◯ Self ◯ Family of Origin ◯ Past Relationships ◯ Current Relationships

Harm Discounting: When we insist that our actions did not cause the level of harm that others say they did. ("I did it, but it is certainly not as bad as you think.") This is another form of playing defense attorney.
Employed by: ◯ Self ◯ Family of Origin ◯ Past Relationships ◯ Current Relationships

Helplessness: When we act incapable or helpless and unable to do things for ourselves, needing others to do them for us.
Employed by: ◯ Self ◯ Family of Origin ◯ Past Relationships ◯ Current Relationships

Impulsiveness: When we can't wait for what we want and do not want to delay our desires, and pursue these desires at the expense of others.

Employed by: ◯ Self ◯ Family of Origin ◯ Past Relationships ◯ Current Relationships

Intention Denial: When we deny our intention for harm. It may be true that we didn't intend to be hurtful or didn't plan a way to control someone else, but that doesn't lessen the impact of our behavior and it is another way of diminishing our responsibility for our actions. ("I didn't mean it" or "Things just got out of control.")

Employed by: ◯ Self ◯ Family of Origin ◯ Past Relationships ◯ Current Relationships

Justice Seeking: When we punish or control others and frame it as punitive toward others because of their behavior toward us. This is another form of playing defense attorney.

Employed by: ◯ Self ◯ Family of Origin ◯ Past Relationships ◯ Current Relationships

Justifying: When we justify our behavior so we don't have to take responsibility. ("I wouldn't have hit you if you hadn't made me so angry.")

Employed by: ◯ Self ◯ Family of Origin ◯ Past Relationships ◯ Current Relationships

Keeping Score: When we explain or justify behavior based on the past actions of others or ourselves. ("I've always done more than you, so it's not a big deal that I didn't do what I said I would this week.")

Employed by: ◯ Self ◯ Family of Origin ◯ Past Relationships ◯ Current Relationships

Lying: When we intentionally state things that are not true, or do not include all details in an attempt to deceive

Employed by: ◯ Self ◯ Family of Origin ◯ Past Relationships ◯ Current Relationships

Making Excuses: Similar to justifying, in that we use it to explain away our behavior rather than hold ourselves accountable. ("I was depressed that day.")

Employed by: ◯ Self ◯ Family of Origin ◯ Past Relationships ◯ Current Relationships

Making Fools of: When we exaggerate the mistakes and weaknesses of others to intentionally demean them and lessen their voice and authority.

Employed by: ◯ Self ◯ Family of Origin ◯ Past Relationships ◯ Current Relationships

Minimizing: When we try to make a behavior seem like it has less impact on those around us. ("At least I only made out with them and didn't sleep with them.")

Employed by: ◯ Self ◯ Family of Origin ◯ Past Relationships ◯ Current Relationships

Mind Reading: When we think we know what other people are thinking and make decisions based on these assumptions, rather than asking.

Employed by: ◯ Self ◯ Family of Origin ◯ Past Relationships ◯ Current Relationships

Ownership: When we feel a sense of ownership of other people, and feel entitled to control their behavior.

Employed by: ◯ Self ◯ Family of Origin ◯ Past Relationships ◯ Current Relationships

Phoniness: When we communicate and apologize insincerely, without fully taking responsibility and without intent to change (maybe just intending to stop getting caught).

Employed by: ◯ Self ◯ Family of Origin ◯ Past Relationships ◯ Current Relationships

Playing Dumb: When we act confused about a situation to avoid responsibility for our behavior, or continuously ask questions that imply we don't understand what others are communicating. ("What did I do? What's wrong with that? What do you mean by that?")

Employed by: ◯ Self ◯ Family of Origin ◯ Past Relationships ◯ Current Relationships

Projecting: When we presume what others are thinking, feeling, or doing based on what we are thinking, feeling, or doing.

Employed by: ◯ Self ◯ Family of Origin ◯ Past Relationships ◯ Current Relationships

Pushing Buttons: When we intentionally use information about another person to get them upset in order to distract from our behavior.

Employed by: ◯ Self ◯ Family of Origin ◯ Past Relationships ◯ Current Relationships

Secretive Behavior: When we hide our activities and omit information to keep people from knowing what we are doing.

Employed by: ◯ Self ◯ Family of Origin ◯ Past Relationships ◯ Current Relationships

Selfish Intent: When we think and act in terms of our needs only, and not the needs of others.

Employed by: ◯ Self ◯ Family of Origin ◯ Past Relationships ◯ Current Relationships

Self-Pitying: When we use statements decrying how bad we are in order to get attention paid to us. ("No one cares about me" or "Everyone would be better off without me around.")

Employed by: ◯ Self ◯ Family of Origin ◯ Past Relationships ◯ Current Relationships

Spiritual/Philosophical Bypassing: When we invoke religion or spirituality over personal responsibility in an attempt to ascribe different meaning to a situation or to avoid doing the work around uncomfortable emotions. ("I'm just turning it over to God" Or "What does any of this mean at a constructivist level, anyway?")

Employed by: ◯ Self ◯ Family of Origin ◯ Past Relationships ◯ Current Relationships

Uniqueness: When we believe that we are unique in such a way that consideration of others (and sometimes rules and laws regarding conduct) do not apply to us in the same way.

Employed by: ◯ Self ◯ Family of Origin ◯ Past Relationships ◯ Current Relationships

Vagueness: When we respond vaguely or unclearly in order to distract from the truth or the content of the conversation.

Employed by: ◯ Self ◯ Family of Origin ◯ Past Relationships ◯ Current Relationships

Victimization Reversal: When we present ourselves as the victim in a scenario, rather than taking responsibility for our role in any events that occurred.

Employed by: ◯ Self ◯ Family of Origin ◯ Past Relationships ◯ Current Relationships

Wearing Down: When we continuously challenge others to give us what we want until they acquiesce out of exhaustion over the continued fighting.

Employed by: ◯ Self ◯ Family of Origin ◯ Past Relationships ◯ Current Relationships

Zero State: Feeling worthless, like nothing, a no-body, and/or empty inside and behaving in ways to help fill that void. This is often where narcissistic behavior stems from.

Employed by: ◯ Self ◯ Family of Origin ◯ Past Relationships ◯ Current Relationships

Questions to consider as you go through this list:

Did you notice any patterns in your answers? Do certain strategies come up time and again?

What strategies have you used on other people?

Do you use different strategies for different people (partners vs. friends vs. family, for example)?

What strategies were used against you in the past? By whom?

What strategies are being used against you in current relationships? By whom?

Are there any patterns that you notice in the strategies you use and the ones used against you?

Are there any patterns that you notice in the strategies that have been used against you in the past and are being used against you in current relationships?

What is one strategy that you have noticed in yourself that you want to commit to changing? How will you do so?

What is one strategy that you have noticed in your current relationships that you are committed to no longer accepting? How will you do so?

Activities for Unfucking Your Communication

In this section, there are several activities to help you unfuck your communication in real life and in real time.

"I" STATEMENTS

Now, here is a great fucking tool for communicating with someone else. You may decide to share these statements with someone. Or you may just be doing internal work around your own communication patterns.

I feel ______________________ when you ______________________

What I want is ______________________

I feel ______________________ when you ______________________

What I want is ______________________

I feel ______________________ when you ______________________

What I want is ______________________

I feel ______________________ when you ______________________

What I want is ______________________

I feel ______________________ when you ______________________

What I want is ______________________

I feel ______________________ when you ______________________

What I want is ______________________

MAP YOUR COMMUNICATION STYLE

Everyone does a little thing known as code-switching. I mean, if I'm chatting with fellow Choctaw people, we may get all rezzy and slangy, but all of us can throw down the professional and academic vocab when the situation requires it. And if we are switching back and forth in terms of the actual words we use, we are definitely changing our communication style in different situations as well. And that isn't always a bad thing, but it does merit awareness. Because sometimes we are adapting our communication style based on our past experiences—and they aren't helpful to our present communication. Think about different people and settings in your life. How do you communicate in these different situations?

Setting/Person	My Communication Style	Example

WHAT YOU WANT, RATHER THAN WHAT YOU DON'T

Cristien Storm's book *Empowered Boundaries* makes the point that while there is nothing inherently bad about a hard no regarding what we don't want, communicating what we do want opens up whole other avenues for dialogue and negotiation. A simple example?

Person 1: How about sushi for dinner?

Person 2, Option 1: Ugh, no.

Person 2, Option 2: I'm really in the mood for a hamburger. I'd like to go there if you are interested? Or we could grab takeout from both places and then we can both get exactly what we are feenin' for.

The second option opens up a completely different conversation and negotiation options.

Below is a template you can use for this purpose:

In this situation, what did the person ask that you want to say no to?

What do you really want in this situation?

How can you lead with that want, rather than just saying no?

HANDLING NO

Nobody likes to be told no. Being told no sucks. It makes our inner toddler kick and scream, and all those toxic societal messages start to leak out in response. But the word *no* (or other words and actions that convey it) is one of the most important ways people express boundaries. What if we started paying attention to "no" messages in a conscious way, and dealt with being told no like badass adults? These are some of the strategies that help:

1. Pay attention to your feelings with self-compassion. If we stuff our feelings, they are just gonna explode out later, like an overstuffed garbage bag. It's ok to think "ow, that hurt . . . I was really wanting that to happen."
2. Put *no* in its proper place. *No* is generally the rejection of your offer, not your personhood. Quite rarely is someone saying that everything about you is wrong and unwanted and fundamentally broken. Our inner demons may tell us that when someone doesn't want to hang out with us, but it's bullshit. There are tons of good humans in the world that I don't want to work with, go to parties with, or see naked. I know you feel the same way . . . and it's important to remember that others can feel that way about you without it being symbolic of something greater.
3. Recognize the boundary you hit and learn from it. If someone tells you no, they are setting a boundary. This is good information about them and your relationship with them. This is the whole point of this book, isn't it? To recognize and communicate and respect boundaries? *No* is the space where we start seeing where the boundaries are erected.
4. Communicate this understanding. Don't wheedle or try to convince. Don't pout around slathered in butthurt. Say "I'm bummed, but I get it, no hard feelings."

In the space below, think of examples of times you didn't handle a no (verbal or nonverbal) as well as you could have and then plan for how you would handle it differently knowing what you know now.

A SITUATION WHERE I REGRET HOW I HANDLED SOMEONE ELSE TELLING ME "NO"	MY ACTION PLAN FOR HANDLING IT DIFFERENTLY NEXT TIME

SAYING NO

One thing that often needs the most practice IRL is saying no. Not with willy-nilly dickitude, but thoughtfully. When someone asks you to do a thing, ask yourself the following questions:

Yes	No	
☐	☐	Are you willing? Is this something you want to do or feel like you should do? Is there meaning in this activity for you?
☐	☐	Are you available? And I don't mean you are running a marathon or anything, but did you have that time set aside for something else? If you planned on being home that evening to catch up on laundry, that is something on your schedule!
☐	☐	Is there any extra information that would sway your decision to yes? Like, did you have laundry planned but a friend has Hozier tickets?

If the answer is no to all of the above, say it. You can say it nicely (my go-to is "I don't have the bandwidth to take that on right now but thanks for thinking of me!"), but say it firmly.

Where did you say no recently?

How was it received?

What was your experience of it?

YOUR BODY'S RESPONSE TO SAYING NO

Try this exercise with another person. The point is to practice learning how your body responds when you agree to something that you don't really want to do, and when you decline to do something you really do want to do. It helps you discover your boundaries within your physical body by listening to the cues. Take note of your reactions and write them down below.

Come up with things that you do and don't want to do with the person you are practicing with. Steer away from anything awful or triggering. Touch can be involved but doesn't have to be. Instead, you can try it with borrowing/using something that belongs to you, or getting closer in someone's space without actually touching.

Authentic Yes	**Inauthentic Yes**	**Authentic No**	**Inauthentic No**

Practice saying yes when you mean it as well as when you don't mean it. Then the same with no" What happens in your body each time? Did you have any "I don't know/I'm not sure/Maybe/I feel confused" experiences? What did those feel like?

THE FEEDBACK BURRITO

One skill I learned in my doc program was how to give feedback to new interns in a way that incorporated all the things they were doing really, really right with the area that we needed to work on. It's slightly more complicated than sandwich feedback (positive, negative, positive), because the human brain centers negative information so strongly (for survival reasons).

This means taking a little extra care in communicating, knowing that brains can be total negativity trolls, by encouraging while also requesting change. Hence the term burrito, because the formula is: positive comment, positive comment, place we need to do a little work, positive comment.

Build Your Own Feedback Burrito:

Positive Comment: I loved it when you did ____________.

Positive Comment: And ____________ was amazing.

Place We Need to Do a Little Work: One thing I think would work better if we did it differently is ____________________. I think it would be even better if we ____________________ instead of ____________________ next time.

Positive Comment: And all in all, I really enjoyed ____________ ____________________________________.

LANGUAGE ELIMINATION

There are certain words and phrases that are just so toxic to communication that they absolutely need to go buh-bye. Let's talk about them and what we can use instead, eh?

"Nothing/I Don't Know"

Do you know when you are so upset that people can see the fumes coming off you? And they ask us what's up and we respond with one of these? It's not helpful. If you aren't sure what's wrong, it's ok to say that. Or if you want to talk about it but you don't want a huge fight, say that too. If your partner uses this language toward you when you ask them what's wrong: don't take the bait. Communicate that you know something is up, and are ready to talk whenever you are.

What You Can Say Instead:

What You Can Say to Someone Who Responds to You Like That:

"Whatever/I Don't Care"

When used against someone, it's dismissive of their experience, right? When it's used about our own emotional content, it's saying, "I don't trust you with the truth." Both are toxic when it comes to resolving a situation. It's ok to say you are overwhelmed and are not sure how to respond if that's the case. And if you DO know and care, speak up! If someone you are communicating with uses these phrases, you can kindly point out that YOU care and are trying to come up with a solution that works for the both of you.

What You Can Say Instead:

What You Can Say to Someone Who Responds to You Like That:

“Always/Never”

Down with all binaries! Gender binaries, orientation binaries, and binary absolutes about the behaviors of others. Be specific about behaviors rather than general, and respond to general accusations with requests for specifics. Point out where things have gotten better or worse. The point is to resolve something, not scream about terribleness, right?

What You Can Say Instead:

What You Can Say to Someone Who Responds to You Like That:

"... but ..."

But negates all good things you said before it. Every time. You did good things times a thousand . . . but . . . you forgot to take the trash out. Far better model? Good thing, good thing, something that you want to work on, finish off with another good thing. And change the BUT to an AND. No matter how nice you are trying to be, brains will dismiss everything before the but!

What You Can Say Instead:

What You Can Say to Someone Who Responds to You Like That:

"You shouldn't feel that way . . ."

Being told how you should feel super sucks. It's just your feelings right? Not right or wrong . . . just IS. And when we are using our "I" statements, we are taking responsibility for them. Even if they are kinda (or really) irrational. They're there. Responding with, "Wow, that's really intense for you . . . " is far more disarming than responding with defensiveness. And if someone criticizes your feelings? Remind them that you are taking responsibility for them, not asking them to.

What You Can Say Instead:

What You Can Say to Someone Who Responds to You Like That:

LISTENING EMPATHETICALLY, OR S.T.F.U.

If we aren't listening effectively, we aren't communicating effectively. I love Sarah Mirk's book *Sex From Scratch: Making Your Own Relationship Rules.* I was skimming through my well-worn copy recently and found a hot-pink highlighted paragraph that really resonates with the ideas I am endeavoring to share here.

Sarah shares a communicating strategy they learned from a tech entrepreneur named Matthew: S.T.F.U. While shutting the fuck up is something that most of us need to do at some point, his acronym is a little different and is wonderful advice for all kinds of communication—because it puts the emphasis on how to listen.

S.T.F.U stands for:

Share Time: Conversation is a two way street. Being silent and listening is just as important a role as talking. A friend of mine actually saw Matthew's talk on this technique and tells me that he offered a math equation to help people conceptualize how to share time in a simple way. He suggests dividing the amount of time you have for the interaction (say an hour) by the number of the people in the room (say six) and make sure you don't spend more than your portion of the time talking (in this case, ten minutes).

Consider: When I have conversations, how do I share time? Is it close to the time divided by the number of people?

Three Seconds: Give others a chance to continue to speak or jump into the conversation before you begin to speak. That means counting to three when there is a pause in the conversation before making your own verbal contribution.

Consider: When I talk with others, is it easy or hard for me to pause for three seconds to allow others to speak? Why?

Find Empathy: Really listen to people . . . not just the content but their backstory. Where are they coming from?

Consider: When I am talking with others, am I aware of the content they are sharing, or am I only listening to reply? What is one small thing I could do to improve in empathy with conversation partners?

Understanding Is Not Necessary: I really love this one. Active listening is designed to help us better understand others, right? But that doesn't mean we always are successful at doing so. We've all had a what-the-literal-fuck moment in regard to someone else's worldview. It's okay to simply accept it as theirs without "getting" it. And maybe further marination on what they are saying will give you an aha moment later?

Consider: When I talk with someone I don't understand, what might it look like to hold space for their experience, even if it is very different from mine?

HA
HA
HA
HA
HA

Activities for Specific Communication Situations

Now that we've covered some of the basics of practical communication, we can take a look at specific challenging communication situations. From politics to religion, boundaries to consent, there's an activity to get you started in saying what you want to say when it's tough.

COMMUNICATING CARE: SPACE, SUPPORT, OR SOLUTIONS

When someone you love is going through it, it can be hard to know how to communicate that you are there for them. One helpful tool is to ask if someone is looking for space, support, or solutions. The following worksheet is designed to walk you through what those things might look like in your life and how you can communicate this kind of care to a struggling loved one.

Here's a basic script:

Space: Do you need to be left alone for some quiet time to process everything . . .

Support: Or would it be more helpful for me to be here with you to listen?

Solutions: And I know you don't need anyone to fix your life, but if you want some help sorting out some options I can do that too.

Consider:

In what kinds of difficult situations do you need space?

Support?

Solutions?

In what specific ways can you communicate care to the people you love by giving them space?

Support?

Solutions?

COMMUNICATING BOUNDARIES

Boundaries and communication go hand in hand. To look at how boundaries are working in your life, consider the following questions:

Which people in your life respect the boundaries that you communicate? What do these people have in common?

Which people do not? What do these people have in common?

If, generally speaking, most people in most situations don't respect your boundaries, then it's time to look at how you are communicating them. Maybe you aren't expressing them as effectively as you thought. (Good news: you can use the activities throughout this workbook to communicate your boundaries more clearly!)

But if you are struggling more in specific relationships or with specific people who keep blowing past your boundaries, then you might, in fact, be dealing with an asshole, or an asshole-infused situation, like a really shitty office culture. Or systemic power-over injustice at a societal level, because let's not pretend that shit doesn't happen.

Before you apply some smackdown, and especially if you're looking at a newer relationship or situation, consider a few other possibilities for why your boundaries aren't being respected:

1. This person could have other stuff going on, such as medical or emotional health issues, that make attending to what you communicate difficult for them.
2. This person might be autistic, making traditional conversation cues difficult for them to suss out.
3. Maybe the individual is neurodiverse in other ways (e.g., ADHD, traumatic brain injury) and has a hard time attending to relational, nonverbal signals and implicit messages.
4. The person could have mental health issues that make them so internally focused that they don't have a real awareness of their impact on others.
5. The person may feel so inferior to you that they don't see how their behavior impacts you.
6. The person's behavioral compulsions could be so ingrained that they use violating the boundaries of others as a means of feeling more in control of the world.
7. This person might be an abuse groomer digging in their heels in an attempt to get you under their emotional coercive control.

If the last scenario is the case, you know what you need to do: get out of there. Seriously, get yourself safe. If it's already escalated to violence, please get some support in making a safety plan. I'd start with the National Domestic Violence Hotline, which you can access by calling 1-800-799-7233 or logging into chat with someone at thehotline.org.

If the other scenarios are a possibility, it's time to have a different conversation. Ask the person how they respond and learn best and try adapting your communication style.

Chances are that with scenarios 1-3, you will need to take away any need for guesswork by expressing your expectations as concretely as pavement. Ask for their attention, express yourself clearly and directly, and elicit feedback regarding their understanding. For example:

Hey, friend person, I need to chat with you about something. I recently had a "well, duh" moment when I realized that I have a boundary that I haven't communicated with you. I'm not mad at you, it's totally on me to have told you. I know you're a hugger, and you hug me whenever we hang out together. And I love that about you. But I grew up in a family where I was forced to hug everyone, whether I was comfortable with it or not. Including some people who really creeped me out. Now I feel more comfortable when people ask if they can hug me before doing so. It's a body autonomy thing that's really important to me. I know that will make sense to you and you will respect that, so I feel comfortable telling you the whole story rather than making up some bullshit story about having a cold and not wanting to hug anyone. In the future, please ask me before you hug me and understand and respect that sometimes the answer will be no, but that has to do with me, not you. Does that make sense? Do you have any questions for me?

In scenarios, 4–6 you may find that responding to them as a high-conflict person is the best course of action. Check out the section later in this workbook on BIFF responses, it's a great tool for high-conflict conversations.

You may be in a situation where you just have to suck it up, too. I'm well aware. You have a shitty job you can't afford to leave. Or you have a shitty family that you can't, at this time, extract yourself from. You have to weigh your options before deciding to throw down over a boundary.

This is another place where the flexibility thing comes in. You will find that tolerating others' lack of respect for your boundaries is far easier to manage when you acknowledge to yourself that you are making a choice to maintain the relationship rather than maintain the boundary. It may be the best choice for you at this moment. Remind yourself that this epic dickitude is just slightly better than the alternative, so you are choosing to accept it for right now. This perspective can really help you tolerate how upset and angry you feel. It may also propel you into creating the action plan you need to extract yourself from an increasingly shitty situation, rather than sitting in that slime pool of disrespect and disregard forever.

Questions for determining if a boundary is safely enforceable:

What kind of relationship do you have with this person (friend, family, coworker, rando at the co-op, etc.)?

Are y'all on the same level or does one of you have power over the other (is someone the boss, has societal privilege, a parent that pays the bills, etc.)?

Is this relationship time-limited (are you stuck with having to deal with this mofo on the regular)?

What would you like to tell this person if you could communicate everything without any consequence?

What are the consequences if you communicate those things?

Are the consequences manageable? Is there a way to make them more manageable?

COMMUNICATING AN APOLOGY

Have you ever been really, really, really fucking sorry about something and when you tried to express it you biffed the apology hardcore? Maybe you were feeling misunderstood and defensive. Or so awkward you fundamentally forgot to use words. I mean, I've done both. Apologizing well takes practice. The good news is, humans fuck up enough to get lots of practice. Here's a formula to practice for next time (or to get the relief of a good apology out of your system when it isn't appropriate to give it directly to the person):

1. Reflect back what the person told or showed you about your actions and the emotions they experienced, to make sure you get it.
2. Take a moment to remind yourself that what they are telling you is not an attack—it's a sign of trust in you and your relationship with them.
3. Acknowledge the harmful impact your words or actions caused them.
4. Thank them for being brave and vulnerable enough to share their experience with you, giving you the opportunity to reflect, take responsibility, and change.
5. Apologize directly and succinctly with direct ownership. (e.g., "I am sorry I did/said . . ." not "I'm sorry you felt/perceived/experienced my actions as . . .")
6. Ask them if there is anything else they need to hear or see from you now or in the future.
7. Thank them for giving you the opportunity to apologize.
8. Accept their response to your apology without argument.
9. Make positive changes in your future interactions so you can make new and different mistakes next time.

Incident for which you'd like to apologize:

Reflect back:

Take a moment:

Acknowledge:

Thank:

Apologize:

Ask:

Thank again:

Accept:

Make positive changes:

Incident for which you'd like to apologize:

Reflect back:

Take a moment:

Acknowledge:

Thank:

Apologize:

Ask:

Thank again:

Accept:

Make positive changes:

Incident for which you'd like to apologize:

Reflect back:

Take a moment:

Acknowledge:

Thank:

Apologize:

Ask:

Thank again:

Accept:

Make positive changes:

Incident for which you'd like to apologize:

Reflect back:

Take a moment:

Acknowledge:

Thank:

Apologize:

Ask:

Thank again:

Accept:

Make positive changes:

Incident for which you'd like to apologize:

Reflect back:

Take a moment:

Acknowledge:

Thank:

Apologize:

Ask:

Thank again:

Accept:

Make positive changes:

Incident for which you'd like to apologize:

Reflect back:

Take a moment:

Acknowledge:

Thank:

Apologize:

Ask:

Thank again:

Accept:

Make positive changes:

COMMUNICATING ABOUT SEXUAL CONSENT

We would save so much time on missed opportunities and hurt feelings if we communicated this information up front, wouldn't we? This worksheet creates a solid framework around those conversations. I suggest filling out your own without a partner around and having them do the same. Then you can share your answers with them, look for overlap, and plan your menu together!

A couple of notes:

1. Don't forget to notate whether you're into giving, receiving, or both. In the "no" category, you can also include off limits parts of your body (no touching of my thighs, no sex with my binder off, etc.)
2. And for the "fantasy" category, make notes on how you would be interested in engaging in sharing that fantasy if you have ideas (dirty talk, erotica, in-person role playing games, online role playing games, watching recorded porn, camming, chaturbation, going to a club, meetup, or party either together or alone that allows viewing, etc.)

What are your sexual orientation descriptive words (pan, bi, gay, straight, grey, ace, demi, stone, etc.)

What are your body part descriptive words (chest, breasts, vulva, vagina, penis, dick, clit, etc)?

What are your gender descriptive words (enby, woman, queer, man, she, he, zie, they, etc)?

What are your relationship descriptive terms (significant other, person I'm dating, partner, boyfriend, girlfriend, umfriend, boo, bae, sweetie, etc.)?

What words do you find triggering, activating, or you really dislike and do not want used to describe you?

Is there anything else around language that a partner would need to know? For example, do you use different words around different people? Are there nicknames others call you that you don't want a partner using? If someone uses descriptive language that your partner knows is on your no-fly list, how do you want them to respond (correct others, let you handle it, etc.)?

COMMUNICATING ABOUT RELIGION: SCRIPT FOR FOR SHITTY COMMENTS

How to deal with shitty comments about religion: this question is one I hear all the time in my world. How the hell DO you respond when Uncle Timmy tells you that God thinks you're an abomination? Without causing a food fight that ends with all the delicious cream-cheese mashed potatoes smashed onto the wall instead of in your belly? Well, with as much calm as possible. Which means preparing your responses ahead of time. Here are some of the scripts I have found most helpful in this type of communication situation.

- That makes God seem kinda an asshole. And I think there is too much beauty and love and grace in the world for that to be the case.
- I think the most important part of religion is the call to love and care for others. Those are the messages I try to focus on in my daily life.
- I guess we won't really know until we get to the Pearly Gates and find out who Peter lets in, eh?
- This is definitely one of those "agree to disagree" moments. Let's move on.
- Oh, you know me . . . just out there making everyone worry about my heathen ass! Thanks for keeping me on your prayer list!

Your turn. Use the following blanks to write down the expected types of shitty comments you expect you might face regarding religion. Then use the above scripts as a template for how to respond.

Shitty Comment: ______________________________

____

Response You Want to Communicate: ______________

____

____

Shitty Comment:

Response You Want to Communicate:

Shitty Comment:

Response You Want to Communicate:

Shitty Comment:

Response You Want to Communicate:

Shitty Comment:

Response You Want to Communicate:

Shitty Comment:

Response You Want to Communicate:

COMMUNICATING ABOUT POLITICS

The baseline for respectful political communication? Express your stance not as an unimpeachable truth (even if it is) and ask the other person about theirs. Then, agree when they're right. Below are some scripts to help you navigate tough political convos.

Other Person: "Your candidate did [insert ungreat thing]."

Your Response: "Yes, I agree. I didn't like that either. I believe in holding all elected officials accountable. That behavior is something that needs to be addressed or rectified." (Or, If necessary, disagree politely: "I saw that same news story and was upset too. But it turns out that situation was misreported, and actually . . .")

Other Person: (states something factually untrue)

Your Response: "I've seen several studies that come to a different conclusion." (Or "That is not a true statement.")

Other Person: (holds unmoving, cult like political beliefs)[1]

Your Response: (use humor) "Not here to talk about that. I came to fight about the Toronto Maple Leafs chances at a Stanley Cup this season. And bruh, what's up with that trade?"

Your turn. Use the following blanks to brainstorm some scripts for specific, difficult communication situations in your life, using the above scripts as inspiration.

Other Person's Dubious Untrue Statement: ______________________

____

Your Response: ______________________________

____

____

1 Presence and understanding, not arguing, are the first steps in deprogramming. The research shows that when people leave cult or cult-like groups or thinking patterns, it was their own disillusionment saying "Waitaminnit." Not the words of friends, families, or therapists. So keep the lines of communication open with safe topics, and you may yet see your loved ones return to reason.

Other Person's Dubious Untrue Statement:

Your Response:

Other Person's Dubious Untrue Statement:

Your Response:

Other Person's Dubious Untrue Statement:

Your Response:

Other Person's Dubious Untrue Statement:

Your Response:

Other Person's Dubious Untrue Statement:

Your Response:

COMMUNICATING ABOUT MENTAL HEALTH/ ADDICTION RECOVERY

You're allowed to get better. And allowed to get better in the ways that make sense to you. Right now, of my clients in recovery, there are multiple paths. A couple are doing a traditional twelve-step model, a couple more prefer Wellbriety, and an equal number are doing moderation management. The variations of supports individuals are using for their mental health treatments are even more diverse. Meds, herbs, ketamine, mushrooms, neurofeedback, other tech, etc. Hell . . . even the type of therapy that I do with them is different based on their needs and preferences. Not everyone wants to do yoga with me, right?

Which is all to say you don't have to defend your journey. You don't have to explain yourself to anyone not paying your bills. I'm proud of you, even if your family isn't. When family members or other loved ones ask intrusive or otherwise ill-advised questions, you can try the following scripts to communicate your needs during your recovery:

Option 1—The Polite Version: I'm working hard on being my healthiest self and it's a personal journey. Thank you for showing your love through your concern, but I'm doing ok and want to focus on the holiday, not this part of my life.

Option 2—The Less-Polite Version: Your questions and comments are both nosey and unkind. None of this is your business and I am asking you to cease these comments and questions or I will leave.

Your turn. Use the following blanks to brainstorm some specific responses to unkind questions about your recovery, using the above scripts as inspiration

Unkind Statement about Recovery: ____________________

____

My Response Option # 1 (The Polite Version): __________

____

My Response Option # 2 (The Polite Version): __________

____

Unkind Statement about Recovery: ______________________

____

My Response Option # 1 (The Polite Version): __________

____

My Response Option # 2 (The Polite Version): __________

____

Unkind Statement about Recovery: ______________________

____

My Response Option # 1 (The Polite Version): __________

____

My Response Option # 2 (The Polite Version): __________

____

Unkind Statement about Recovery: ______________________

____

My Response Option # 1 (The Polite Version): __________

____

My Response Option # 2 (The Polite Version): __________

____

Unkind Statement about Recovery: ______________________

____

My Response Option # 1 (The Polite Version): __________

____

My Response Option # 2 (The Polite Version): __________

____

COMMUNICATING ABOUT FOOD

Food plays such a big role in our lives, so it makes sense that communicating about it can be such an undertaking. Especially when we consider that the number of people who are living with/working to heal from an eating disorder (or disordered eating) is large. Research says about 30 million people, and that's likely an artificially low number, only a count of people who have met official diagnostic criteria and are actively seeking help.

Most everyone in industrialized society has had a toxic relationship with food at some point in their lives. The average American will be on an average of 126 diets in their lifetime. Which is one of those numbers that is so nuts to me and so telling about how toxic our culture is.

And the stressors that influence our eating patterns, at least in the short term? Two big ones are experiencing conflict and feeling lonely. And many people find these issues compounded by "well-meaning" comments about our appearance, what we are eating or not eating, or any other sensitive subjects (especially those that are identity-driven). And our dietary patterns do affect our mental health.

Please consider how you best handle stressful situations, and try to create some pockets of that self-care for this situation. You can use the following questions to begin the journey of finding that support in your own life, forging a new way of communication around food:

Do you have any peers or other loved ones—who know the journey of disordered eating—that you can call or text if you are in danger of restricting, binging, or punching the shit out of any family members that want to comment on your body?

Who are some allies you can enlist at fraught gatherings? (For example, having a cousin jump in and say to Uncle Chuck, "Oh, we're not talking about people's bodies this year, Chuck, let it go." And then you can say, "Hey, Uncle Chuck, I heard you caught some amazing walleye last month on your fishing trip . . . what's your secret?")

COMMUNICATING ABOUT MONEY

Financial conversations can be stressful and triggering and quickly turn into fights. It helps to bring your best self to the table instead of your scared, defensive, and reactionary self. Because in the end, it should be you two vs. the problem instead of you two vs. each other.

THINK is a "best self" skill you can use in all sorts of financial conversations: with family, partners, your boss, your landlord, the bank teller, even with yourself. It comes from a theoretical orientation I borrow from on the regular, dialectical behavioral therapy. Developed by Marsha Linehan to help individuals with borderline personality disorder (BPD) better self-regulate, it matches traditional cognitive techniques with mindfulness and distress tolerance based skills.

Since developed, it's been shown to be effective in many different situations. And one of the core areas that DBT focuses on is interpersonal effectiveness. That is, maintaining a clear understanding of our own boundaries, and attending to our wants and needs, while respecting the other person and the relationship itself. DBT is a skills-based approach that uses a lot of acronyms to help frame the skills.

One of the interpersonal effectiveness skills I use often is the THINK skill, because it is specifically designed as a tool to not only communicate effectively with a partner, but also keep from dumping a ton of negative emotions into the conversation even when upset. Like every skill, it's easier to practice using it before you're in a negative place. After a while it will become second nature to communicate using THINK, which will make arguments far easier to manage.

T stands for "Think." Yup, super original. But hey, the thoughtful part of our brain can shut down when we are upset. And in this case it means think of the other person's perspective on the issue. Where are they coming from? Do they see it in a different way from you?

H stands for "Have Empathy." Empathy is different from sympathy. It doesn't mean "feel sorry for," it means really connecting to the other person's emotional experience. Remember to connect to their emotional content, not just your own.

I stands for "Interpret Their Behavior." And let your imagination take over. You can start with the most irrational, ridiculous thing possible ("They totally schemed to fuck me over . . . it is part of their master, evil plan of world domination!") to the more reasonable ("Their behavior wasn't thoughtful, but it wasn't intentionally hurtful"). Starting with the most extreme seems counterintuitive, but it burns off some steam and helps connect us to how overreactive we can be when upset . . . which allows us to more easily accept a rational interpretation.

N stands for "Notice." This means simply notice how the other person is responding and interacting. Notice when they are trying to make improvements. Notice their reaction to you. Notice the other things going on in their life that are operating as either positives or negatives. Pay attention to where they are at, not just where you are at.

K stands for "Kindness." Even if you are having to make a hard decision or hold firm to a boundary doesn't mean you have to be mean, right? And honestly, consistency and firmness are also forms of kindness. And you can express that in words, as well as actions. "Fuck off and leave me alone" isn't kind. But "I'm not going anywhere, and I know we will work through this, but right now I need some time to calm down so we can discuss it more effectively" is kind. It maintains commitment and attachment, and expresses a needed boundary and break from a difficult situation, while taking responsibility for the need.

COMMUNICATING IN SYSTEMS

You know what this means. Business settings, school settings, government agencies, on the phone with the electric company trying to keep your power turned on until you get paid on Friday. The stuff where speaking fancy can help you get what you want.

There's a concept from business communication research that can be helpful here: the differences between horizontal and vertical communication.

Possible dirty connotations on first glance aside, horizontal communication just means talking with your colleagues. Our language in these situations tends to remain informal. For example, if you are assigned the same shift as a work buddy, you can totally say something like, "Bestie, respectfully, not happening, I'm swamped AF over here" when they ask for help with their shift tasks.

By contrast, vertical communication, in the business world, is top-down communication. And this is where we are far more likely to communicate formally. When a supervisor tells you to help them with their shift tasks? The response is prolly gonna be different as in: "This is what I have on my task list for today. If I help you with yours, we will need to reprioritize my workload to make room. How would you like to reorganize our deliverables?"

This section focuses on vertical communication, expanding the definition to any situation where someone has more power than you. Or at least a level of power that you are wanting to access for your benefit. So not just your boss or professor. But also the clerk at your local government office or the nice lady at the electric company you are trying to convince to give you three more days to pay your bill. Or the frazzled barista that has been fending off Karen bullshit all day that you want to convince to remake your drink.[2]

These interactions also fall under the domain of vertical communication. Which we have all been culturally trained to formal-

2 The customer is always right—in matters of taste. We don't usually include those last four words. If someone wants their house painted with zebra stripes. It's their house and their taste, not the painter's business. If they want it painted for free? That's the painter's business.

ize. While that is changing (very slowly), being able to speak with more formality greatly enhances your chances of getting shit done when navigating top-down systems. Knowing the rules helps you better decide when to break them, after all.

Context aside, all business/organizational communication has one or more of the following three goals: instrumental, relational, or identity.

Instrumental goals use communication to complete an objective. (Communication in service of getting shit done, so to speak.)

Relational goals help strengthen or weaken our relationships in the workplace.

Identity goals shape how someone is perceived.

Now, communication researchers say more than one goal could be in place at a time. And I would say, for peak effectiveness of getting shit done, all three goals should be in place all the time. If we are trying to accomplish a goal. Say, using the example of getting three days grace on your light bill, giving you time to get you paid and make a payment before it is turned off? When you call in to make your case, your goal of getting the grace period is better served if the customer service rep likes you and perceives you as a good and deserving person.

Let's face it, humans are judgmental motherfuckers. We are always sorting our fellow humans in the categories. We can work hard at overcoming these judgments, or at least trying our damndest to base them on facts instead of stereotypes and vibes. But our tendency to judge is a reality of our survival-based primitive brains.

So let's use the three-day extension example.

Customer Service Rep: Good morning, this is Rowan. How can I help you today?

Me: Good morning! I really need a three-day extension on my power disconnect notice. I get paid on Friday and can pay it then!

Customer Service Rep: I'm sorry, we have sent you multiple notices over the past two months. That was the final notice.

Now this is a perfectly polite request, right? It wasn't shitty or Karen-y. The focus was instrumental. And the request was declined, equally politely and accurately to the situation. Still, I can't not have power for the week and I have to find ways to get up and go to work anyway. And now I have to pay to have everything turned back on, as well as late fees and the bill itself. And I don't have enough money to do all of that. So what happens if we add relational and identity strategies to this situation?

Customer Service Rep: Good morning, this is Rowan. How can I help you today?

Me: Rowan, good morning! This is Faith Harper, and I am really hoping you can help me figure something out. I apologize if I sound stressed and anxious. You have nothing to do with it, but I am super stressed and anxious about my shut-off notice, and I am sure you can hear it in my voice.

Rowan: Thanks for that, I've been there too. What's up?

Me: I lost my job a couple months ago. I just started a new one, which is great but I don't get paid until Friday. I am hella behind on my light bill and that's on me, but I am finally starting to get caught up, I'm working all the overtime I can get! Are there any options or programs to extend my shut-off notice for three more days so I can pay it as soon as my direct deposit hits on Friday?

Rowan: Been there too! We don't have a ton of options in that regard, but I can tell you there is a law that prevents us from turning off your power if you have a medical issue that requires you to have power. Like if you use a medical device that has to be plugged in?

Me: I have asthma, does that count?

Rowan: That is definitely a condition that can be exacerbated by the heat! It isn't always approved, your doctor will have to fill stuff out. But I can mark you down as applying for that program and send you the forms. They won't turn off your power for a bit, expecting you to send in the forms for REAP assistance. That will buy you time, and honestly, not a bad thing to actually apply for in case you ever need help in the future.

Me: Rowan, you are a lifesaver!

Rowan: Happy to help! Is there anything else I can assist you with?

Me: Can you patch me through to your supervisor? They always hear complaints, and I'd love to make sure you get your flowers for saving my ass. I'd like to at least leave them a nice message about your quality customer service? What's your last name?

This may seem excessive, and likely extra effort for something that won't work. But as an official old person who uses these strategies, I can safely tell you these strategies *almost always do* work. This conversation creates a relationship, in which you recognize the humanity and the role of the person answering the phone, knowing this is someone who tends to see some of the worst of human behavior. YOU also take responsibility for both the fact that you are behind on your bill and you are upset that you may lose services, instead of being defensive and argumentative . . . while showing the steps you are taking to get caught up.

(And yes, I entirely agree that every human being should have what they need to live . . . that was the point of creating society. Everyone is deserving of food, shelter, and all other material supports. But that isn't an argument that works well in call centers. You really do have to demonstrate that you are especially deserving of Rowan's support. Then you show them they were right to do so, by making sure their boss knows they provided great customer service.)

But like all communication, working with systems is complex. Since there isn't a formal recipe, here are some ideas I want you to take from this:

Treat all people like people. Pay attention to someone's name and use it when appropriate.[3] You made the convo person to person . . . not person to entity-representative. Also, if you have a visual (in-person, on video chat, or whatever), you can find other things to notice and comment on. I swear I got assistance swing-

3 Don't do the weird saying their name over and over car-dealer-salesman shit. Be authentic and human in your use of someone's name.

ing some extra financial aid in my doc program, just by complimenting the necklace of the lady in the bursar's office. It doesn't have to be slavish fluffing, either.

It's just noticing.

If we are using the "remake my drink" example, you may say something to the barista like, "I can see you're slammed and working your ass off. I'm so sorry to add more to your workload, but can you remake this for me? I hate being that person, but it didn't come out the way it usually does." That's noticing. We are recognizing and connecting to the humanity of others. Not treating them like NPCs in our personal universe.

Also? If you are really trying to get something done, you should be keeping notes. Like I do when I have to contact federal financial aid (necklace lady hooked me up, but I still gotta pay it back). I write down the name of the person I am talking to, the date, and the important points of the interaction for my own records. Again, names matter!

And having their name lets you go back and give them their flowers when they do help you. And I don't mean dangle it over their heads like, "Help me and I'll give you a baller Yelp review." Do it because it is the right thing to do. Do it because hardly anyone ever does that. When I took an extra eight minutes to praise a postal worker to her supervisor last year, it was because she helped me get my passport in time. I won't need another passport for ten years, so it isn't like I'm gonna need to lean on her again. But the financial aid lady? Whose supervisor got an email from me hyping her up? I got the financial aid I needed, no questions asked, for the rest of my time in grad school. So, yes, bonus points. Either way, you will have an ally if you need one again later.

(Too bad I can't talk my way out of paying it all back, or I'd give that a go too.)

The more attention you pay in these scenarios, the better you will get at reading the person you are interacting with. Sometimes a quiet introvert responds to less energy, and you being soft-spoken and giving them space keeps them from being overwhelmed. But sometimes you'll find one in the wild that responds well to a bit of extrovert adoption energy—making them a friend by cracking a few jokes (not at their expense!) and building up the relational goal part of the process. If you are building the relational goal up to that point, then the conversation is more horizontal and you can be more informal.

Again, it's more a vibe than a recipe, but keeping in mind the three goals and attempting to tag in all of them can make a big difference in getting stuff done.

Now it's your turn. Use the below blanks to come up with scripts for different systems you may encounter and communicate within, using the three goals: instrumental, relational, and identity.

System You Are Communicating In: ____________________

Instrumental Goal: What do you want to get done through this conversation?

Relational Goal: What can you do to strengthen the relationship you have with the human representing this system?

Identity Goal: How can you lift up the human you are communicating with (for example, speaking well of them to their supervisor)?

System You Are Communicating In: ____________________

Instrumental Goal: What do you want to get done through this conversation?

Relational Goal: What can you do to strengthen the relationship you have with the human representing this system?

Identity Goal: How can you lift up the human you are communicating with (for example, speaking well of them to their supervisor)?

System You Are Communicating In: ______________________

Instrumental Goal: What do you want to get done through this conversation?

Relational Goal: What can you do to strengthen the relationship you have with the human representing this system?

Identity Goal: How can you lift up the human you are communicating with (for example, speaking well of them to their supervisor)?

COMMUNICATING IN GROUPS

So you want to organize a workshop, a *platica* (a Spanish word you see a lot in my part of the country to define community discussion looking to facilitate change and understanding) or another community conversation. Badass!

This kind of conversation can have a lot of benefits.

It can also have a lot of pitfalls. I've seen such talks go off the rails, and you probably have too. Being proactive from the beginning with a structure to help you accomplish your goals can really help. Rules can also help. If you are organizing a platica, start with solid ground rules laying out these expectations so the real vulnerability of this work can shine through and change can unfold.

Example Rules:

- Communicate using "I" statements (e.g., "I feel . . ." rather than "You made me . . ."
- Speak from personal experience, rather than speaking for the experience of others, unless expressly and specifically asked to do so. ("My friend could not be here tonight but asked me to read this out loud to the group about their experience.")

- Speaking will be limited to XX minutes to allow everyone a chance to participate. Individuals who would like to speak can sign up on the board up front (or we will speak in turn in a circle, etc.)
- Individuals who do not wish to speak can either verbally comment "pass" or shake their head no when it is their turn or they are questioned. Alternatively, seating can be arranged in such a way that individuals who do not wish to speak can sit in a different area.
- There is not any required participation in experiential exercises.
- Any exercises that are done on paper (journaling, completing worksheets . . . like any of the worksheets earlier on in this workbook, for example) are not required to be shared out loud.

COMMUNICATING WITH YOURSELF

Perhaps the most basic form of communication in our lives is our communication with ourselves. Our own dumb brains communicate a lot of things—including some really negative shit. And for those of us who didn't grow up in the greatest of circumstances often have internalized unkind voices from our past as our own. All my clients will laugh knowingly at the following statement, because when they are talking ugly to themselves about themselves? I ask,

Whose voice is that?

And they will always say, "Mine!" And I respond, "Sure, it is now. But the brain doesn't start out being so nasty to itself. Before it became your internal dialogue, whose external dialogue was that? Who talked to you like that?" And it was a childhood parent or caretaker every time—the people entrusted to nourish and care for and grow our small little bodies and brains into loving and competent adults. So many kids didn't have their bodies abused growing up, but did have their hearts and minds abused with this kind of correction. And as we grow up, that voice becomes our internal voice.

Now, these voices are our thoughts. And they are referred to as automatic thoughts or automatic negative thoughts—or ANTS—for a reason. They are wired in so young that they happen instantaneously. And that's ok. We aren't responsible for our first thoughts. They are as immediate as touching a hot stove and yanking our hands away. You are, however, responsible for your second thoughts and your first behavior. Capturing the ANTS and reframing them using cognitive-behavioral therapy will help you pivot to a more skillful behavior (instead of a vagal-activated fight/flight/freeze response).

Here is how it works. When you catch yourself saying something toxic (and yes, you can totally do this on paper or in the notes app on your phone), note it and then consider either a more accurate or at least a more balanced, helpful message. An **alternate** message challenges the original toxic message entirely. A **balanced** message acknowledges a fundamental truth, while focusing on managing it in a more empowering way.

Toxic Self-Talk: OMG, I am such a dumbass, I can't do **anything** right!

Alternate Response: I wish I had done better. But, hey, I'm really good at learning from my mistakes and trying again. Let me think about a different approach to this problem. And for the record, there are plenty of things I get right!

Toxic Self-Talk: I really like that person and they have no interest in me at all. I must really suck.

Balanced Response: I've tried making a connection and I'm not their cup of tea. Or they have other stuff going on and don't have space for me in their life right now. I'm going to focus my time and attention on the people who are interested in spending time with me so I can remember that there are plenty of people who think I'm a fantastic cup of tea!

Alternate and balanced responses are both designed to be more gentle, and self-compassionate in the face of a nasty inner dialogue. If the message is just plain wrong, tell yourself that. If it is fairly accurate but simplified and self-recriminatory, then you shift it to something that is more complex and complete to the situation. Because we aren't looking to self-gaslight, just to be as fair and considerate to ourselves as we would someone else.

You can use the following blanks to capture and reframe some ANTS in your life. What are some examples of toxic self-talk statements you say to yourself? Once you write those down in the blanks below, try coming up with an alternate response and a balanced response for each one.

Pro-tip: If you need help coming up with an alternate and/or balanced response, consider the following questions.

- What did I feel when the ANT came into my head? How did I want to feel?
- What evidence in my life supports the ANT? What evidence counters the ANT?
- What would I say to a friend going through the same thing?
- What would I like to change about my actions in relationship to this ANT?
- What realistic and kind things can I say to myself to encourage me to act in the way I want to when this ANT pops into my head?

Toxic Self-Talk: ____

____

Alternate Response (challenges the original toxic message entirely): ____

____

____

Balanced Response (acknowledges a fundamental truth in the original message, while focusing on managing it in a more empowering way): ____

____

____

Toxic Self-Talk: ____

____

Alternate Response (challenges the original toxic message entirely): ____

____

____

Balanced Response (acknowledges a fundamental truth in the original message, while focusing on managing it in a more empowering way): ____

____

____

Toxic Self-Talk: ____

____

Alternate Response (challenges the original toxic message entirely): ____

____

____

Balanced Response (acknowledges a fundamental truth in the original message, while focusing on managing it in a more empowering way): ____

____

____

Toxic Self-Talk: ____________________

____

Alternate Response (challenges the original toxic message entirely): ____________________

____

____

Balanced Response (acknowledges a fundamental truth in the original message, while focusing on managing it in a more empowering way): ____________________

____

____

Toxic Self-Talk: ____________________

____

Alternate Response (challenges the original toxic message entirely): ____________________

____

____

Balanced Response (acknowledges a fundamental truth in the original message, while focusing on managing it in a more empowering way): ____________________

____

____

Toxic Self-Talk: ____________________

____

Alternate Response (challenges the original toxic message entirely): ____________________

____

____

Balanced Response (acknowledges a fundamental truth in the original message, while focusing on managing it in a more empowering way): ____________________

____

____

Activities for Communicating through Conflict

Conflict is one of the trickiest communication situations—that's why it gets a whole section in this workbook. But it is possible to communicate even in the most difficult conflict, and the activities in this section are here to empower you to say what you need to, no matter what.

BEFORE CONFLICT: WHO DO I WANT TO BE IN THE WORLD?

A big part of communicating effectively—especially through conflict— is operating from your own moral center. Meaning, you act from a place that is congruent with the kind of person you want to be in the world. Even though everything we do and every interaction we have should operate from this place, we rarely think about what that really looks like.

Circle ten adjectives that describe what you are like. Try to be as honest and accurate as possible; this is a snapshot of where you are in the present. Rank them one through ten from most significant to least in describing your personality.

Aimless	Content	Disorganized	Hard-working	Kind	Outgoing	Sad	Strong
Anxious	Depressed	Energetic	Helpful	Lazy	Plain	Serious	Unhelpful
Careless	Disengaged	Funny	Honest	Optimistic	Purposeful	Shy	
Centered	Dishonest	Happy	Intelligent	Organized	Relaxed	Stressed	

Now pick up a different color pen and choose ten items to describe your personal ideal. Not what other people wish for you but what you truly wish for yourself. This can be difficult if you are used to letting others guide your path. So listen to your gut over your head. Now rank those ten from most to least important. Now compare the colors. Where do they match up? Where are you out of alignment? Is any of your stuckness related to not being in alignment with your core identity?

Now, use the following questions as journal prompts to create a check-in space for making sure your communication lines up with your values.

What do you want to stand for? What do you believe in?

What personal attributes and positive characteristics do you want to demonstrate to yourself and others in the world?

How will you know when you are successfully living your values?

How will you know if you aren't?

How will you know if your priorities have changed and you need to recalibrate?

BEFORE CONFLICT: RELATIONAL IMAGES

Relational images are how we expect other people to react to us when we say something. These images are things we consider to be core truths about the world. Whether or not they are empirically true, we operate like they are. Which means that these rules we create about our relationships can hold us down from living a fulfilling and authentic life more than anything else because we are always so worried about how others will respond to our authenticity. Ask yourself the same question and see if anything comes up for you in the same way.

If I say . . .

Other people will . . .

If I say . . .

Other people will . . .

If I say . . .

Other people will . . .

If I say . . .

Other people will . . .

If I say . . .

Other people will . . .

What surprised you doing this exercise?

Did you uncover some "truths" that you didn't realize you were operating from?

How are they affecting your relationships?

What do you want to focus on changing?

CONFLICT COMMUNICATION QUESTION CHECK-IN

Even the world's best communicators still have conflict. If the goal was never to have conflict, that would be easy. You would just have to be a total doormat and give people whatever they want all the time. But if you don't want to be a doormat, the goal isn't conflict avoidance, but conflict management.

When things go sideways in your communication in a conflict, consider the following questions:

- **Is the source of the communication intentional?** Is the other person intentionally fucking with you? Or is this a miscommunication?
- **Who are you really mad at?** Are you stressed about other situations not related to this conflict? If so, how can you decompress before returning to the conversation?
- **How can you use humor—rather than sniping—in this situation?** Where does your humor overlap with the other person's? If appropriate, how can you use that shared sense of humor to talk about the issue in question?
- **How can you say what you want to without contempt for the other person?** How can you avoid the four destructive horseman of relationships[4]: criticism, defensiveness, stonewalling, and contempt?
- **What are your needs vs. preferences in this situation?** Where is the overlap with the other person's needs and preferences? Is this situation impacting needs or preferences?

Below are some spaces to use when you're facing specific conflicts in your life and you need a check-in with the above questions before making your next move.

4 Thanks, John Gottman.

- What is the conflict?

- Who is the conflict with?

- Is the source of the communication intentional on the other person's part?

- Who (or what) are you really mad at right now?

- How can you use humor—rather than sniping—in this situation?

- How can you say what you want to without contempt for the other person?

- What are your needs vs. preferences in this situation?

- What is the conflict?

- Who is the conflict with?

- Is the source of the communication intentional on the other person's part?

- Who (or what) are you really mad at right now?

- How can you use humor—rather than sniping—in this situation?

- How can you say what you want to without contempt for the other person?

- What are your needs vs. preferences in this situation?

- What is the conflict?

- Who is the conflict with?

- Is the source of the communication intentional on the other person's part?

- Who (or what) are you really mad at right now?

- How can you use humor—rather than sniping—in this situation?

- How can you say what you want to without contempt for the other person?

- What are your needs vs. preferences in this situation?

- What is the conflict?

- Who is the conflict with?

- Is the source of the communication intentional on the other person's part?

- Who (or what) are you really mad at right now?

- How can you use humor—rather than sniping—in this situation?

- How can you say what you want to without contempt for the other person?

- What are your needs vs. preferences in this situation?

DEAR MAN: OBJECTIVE EFFECTIVENESS

Objective effectiveness is a term used in dialectical behavioral therapy to break down how we can best get what we want in a relationship. The acronym DEAR MAN is a great mnemonic for remembering the best ways to be effective without being a manipulative shithead. For each letter in the acronym, write down an example of when you used it this week and how it made you feel.

Describe: Clearly and concretely say what you want. Even people who know us super well don't read minds, you know?

Express: Share your emotions while taking responsibility for them. "I feel . . . when you . . . " is far more effective that "you made me mad."

Assert: Being assertive isn't dickitude, it's honesty. "I don't know if I'm feeling up to it" is a hint, but "I'm exhausted and want to skip the party this evening" is assertive.

Reinforce: When people do the thing you ask them to do, thank them!

Mindful: Don't get sidetracked by off-topic disagreements. Stick to what issue you are trying to resolve.

Appearance: Demonstrate confidence in how you present yourself. Even if your words are assertive, people are less likely to take you seriously if your body language isn't.

Negotiate: Be open to compromise—relationships are give and take.

BIFF STATEMENTS

A powerful tool for communicating in conflict situations is the BIFF Response (Brief, Informative, Friendly, and Firm) and by avoiding the three As (Advice, Admonishment, and Apologies). These are tools from Bill Eddy's High Conflict Institute that I teach to people on the regular. They are great tools for handling conflict and also with situations that are emotionally charged in general.

If you are in the process of establishing and holding better boundaries with someone for the first time, it's going to feel emotionally charged since it's all weird and awkward and new for everyone involved. Having a bit of a recipe will help a ton. Try this one. (Add extra garlic if you're feeling sassy.)

Brief: Don't give any extra info. Don't over-explain. The more you write or say, the more fodder you are giving the aggrieved party for their battle, yeah? Let's say you got an angry missive from your boss, accusing you of jacking the keys to the dumpster. Instead of writing an eight-paragraph defense, try a brief, factual response: "I clocked out two hours before closing last Thursday, so I didn't carry out the garbage that day and I never used the keys."

Informative: Don't focus on their incorrect statements, focus on your accurate ones. No sarcasm, no negging, no remarks about the other person's personality, ethical choices, etc. We are looking to end the conflict, not throw down about who the real dumbass in this scenario is. In the same work example, you might add the information, "In order to refresh my memory, I double checked the calendar. I wasn't the person who closed that day, it was Xander."

Friendly: I know, it doesn't seem fair that you have to be nice when someone else is showing their ass. The best way of coming out of the conflict unscathed is to not match hostility with hostility. This doesn't mean fake nicey-nice—just civil. You are far more likely to get a neutral response, if not a positive one. Going back to the work example, you could phrase it as something like,

"Hi, Sarah! Xander and I did both work last Thursday, but I clocked out early because it was so slow and Xander closed by themself, so I don't know where the keys to the dumpster ended up."

Firm: Be firm without being threatening. Don't make comments that can invite more discussion (e.g., "Let me know if you have any questions" or "I hope you agree that . . . "). Back to Xander the key-stealer? You could close with "I wish I could be of more help, hopefully Xander will be." Think like Forrest Gump. As in "that's all I have to say about that." If you need to get a decision from someone and can't end the discussion here, another feature of "firm" is offering two choices so you don't have continued over-discussion.

If you get more communication after you have already BIFFed your response, you can either ignore it or broken-record your BIFF response with the same key words and even less content until they give up.

Another Bill Eddy trick for BIFF communication is to avoid the three As: Advice, Admonishments, and Apologies. So let's look at those, as well:

Advice: You don't want to give anyone advice on how to manage themselves or the situation they are ramped up about. They are already hot under the collar so you won't get anywhere. I know I don't hear much when I'm butthurt—that's a pretty universal response. Notice that rather than telling Sarah to check the timecards in my example, I said "I double checked the calendar and confirmed . . . " That avoided giving her advice on how to do her job. She will realize she should have done so herself once she calms down, so it's all good.

Admonishments: You may want to offer corrective feedback, but just like advice-giving, this isn't the time. The point of a BIFF response is to defuse an emotional conversation and end it for the time being. So avoid anything that makes it sound like you are explaining their behavior to them like they are a naughty child. Again, with Sarah the manager, imagine the continued battle if you had said, "If you had acted like an actual manager, you would have checked the schedule before having a ragefit at me"???

Apologies: Authentic apologies are a good thing. But when everyone is activated is not the time for them. Apologizing can give the other person something to blame us for, extending the conversation. "I'm so sorry I don't know what happened to the keys" can let Sarah continue to blame you for her ridiculous insistence that you are somehow responsible. A more gentle "social apology" can be helpful to diffuse the issue, if you want to add that to the mix, however. "I'm so sorry you are having to deal with such a frustrating situation with everything else on your plate" is a show of commiseration and empathy that doesn't connect you to the blame game and doesn't give Sarah any more ammo.

Practice having a difficult conversation (it can be totally made-up) with a friend. Or if you are doing this as a group exercise, break up in pairs and take turns. If you are using this workbook to check in with your own communication style, you can pull up an old email, DM, or text where you had to set a boundary with someone.

Upon reviewing the conversation, did you use BIFF? Did you avoid the three As? If you didn't get them all down, no worries. Use the space below to write out an alternative response that covers the parts you missed.

Yeah, I know it feels weird and dumb, but if you create a new communication pathway in your brain, it's far easier to access that pathway when you are dealing with some upset, pushy human in the future.

- ◌ Brief
- ◌ Informative
- ◌ Friendly
- ◌ Firm
- ◌ No Advice
- ◌ No Admonishments
- ◌ No Apologies

Rewind and pick up the pieces you missed by . . .

Conclusion: Where We've Been

This last section is about activities that allow you to combine the various skills you've learned throughout this workbook and connect them to your specific circumstances.

MISCOMMUNICATION LOG

Sometimes things just go badly in the moment when we're trying to communicate clearly. This log is to give you a space to reflect on those sideways communication times and how to make similar situations go better in the future.

Miscommunication

• *What happened?*

• *What went wrong?*

• *What would you do differently in the future?*

Miscommunication

- *What happened?*

- *What went wrong?*

- *What would you do differently in the future?*

Miscommunication

- *What happened?*

- *What went wrong?*

- *What would you do differently in the future?*

Miscommunication

• *What happened?*

• *What went wrong?*

• *What would you do differently in the future?*

Miscommunication

- *What happened?*

- *What went wrong?*

- *What would you do differently in the future?*

Miscommunication

- *What happened?*

- *What went wrong?*

- *What would you do differently in the future?*

Miscommunication

• *What happened?*

• *What went wrong?*

• *What would you do differently in the future?*

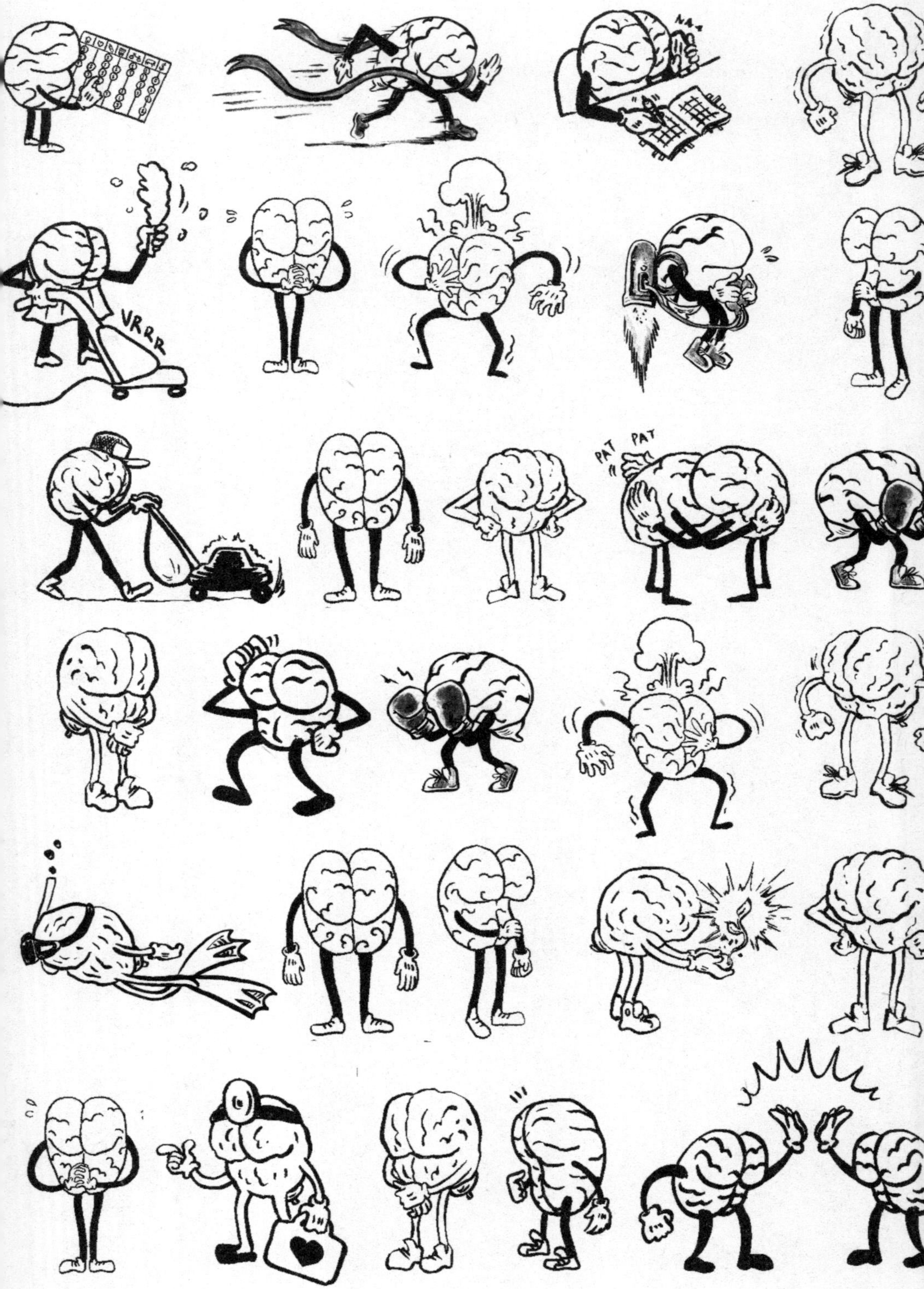
VRRR
PAT PAT

GOLD FUCKING (COMMUNICATION) STARS

You know what I miss from childhood? Gold stars. People recognizing the effort I put into something. Here's a worksheet so you can give gold stars to yourself for your healthy, everyday communication achievements.

Gold Fucking Star	The Thing I Tried	How I Felt Before I Tried the Thing (0–10)	How I Felt After I Tried the Thing (0–10)	My General Feelings About the Thing (0–10)
☆				
☆				
☆				
☆				
☆				
☆				
☆				
☆				
☆				

CHECK-IN: WHAT'S NEXT?

Whew! That was a lot of work around communication, and I'm fucking proud of you. Why? Because even when communicating solely for the benefit of someone else, we are participating in our own healing. Recognizing we can be kind and skillful and proactive even when distressed? That shit helps us recognize our own self-worth as well as the inherent worth of every being around us. Good communication helps heal trauma. And we deserve any strategies we can get our hands on when doing this work.

Healthier relationships? Firm, kind boundaries in the face of fuckery? Treating people like people with their own struggles and complexities? Those are all markers of a healed soul. And we all deserve one.

Take some time to flip through this workbook and all the work you've done through it.

What tools stuck out to you?

What is one thing about communication that surprised you that you learned along the way?

What tools do you have more questions about?

Since beginning this workbook, what's already changed in your communication style?

What communication situations do you feel more confident in now?

What else do you want to work on in your communication going forward?

ABOUT THE AUTHOR

Dr. Faith G. Harper, ACS, ACN, holds postdoctoral certifications in sexology and applied clinical nutrition and is trained in yoga, meditation, breathwork, mindful movement, and all of those other forms of care that make most people avoid her at parties (though she promises to never make you do a down-dog). In the past, she has worked in academia, community mental health, and private practice as a licensed professional counselor and currently defines her practice as a clinical coaching specialist. She maintains a connection with academia through her work with the Society of Indian Psychologists. She lives in San Antonio, TX, with her amazing friends and family and terrible rescue cats. She can be reached through her website, faithgharper.com.

MORE BY DR. FAITH

Books

The Autism Partner Handbook (with Joe Biel and Elly Blue)
The Autism Relationships Handbook (with Joe Biel)
Befriend Your Brain
Coping Skills
How to Be Accountable (with Joe Biel)
This Is Your Brain on Depression
Unfuck Your Addiction
Unfuck Your Adulting
Unfuck Your Anger
Unfuck Your Anxiety
Unfuck Your Blow Jobs
Unfuck Your Body
Unfuck Your Boundaries
Unfuck Your Brain
Unfuck Your Cunnilingus
Unfuck Your Friendships
Unfuck Your Grief
Unfuck Your Intimacy
Unfuck Your Stress
Unfuck Your Worth
Unfuck Your Writing (with Joe Biel)
Woke Parenting (with Bonnie Scott)

Workbooks

Achieve Your Goals
The Autism Relationships Workbook (with Joe Biel)
How to Be Accountable Workbook (with Joe Biel)
Unfuck Your Anger Workbook
Unfuck Your Anxiety Workbook
Unfuck Your Body Workbook
Unfuck Your Boundaries Workbook
Unfuck Your Intimacy Workbook
Unfuck Your Worth Workbook
Unfuck Your Year

Zines

The Autism Handbook (with Joe Biel)
BDSM FAQ
Dating
Defriending
Detox Your Masculinity (with Aaron Sapp)
Emotional Freedom Technique
Getting Over It
How to Find a Therapist
How to Say No
Indigenous Noms
Relationshipping
The Revolution Won't Forget the Holidays
Self-Compassion
Sex Tools
Sexing Yourself
STI FAQ (with Aaron Sapp)
Surviving
This Is Your Brain on Addiction
This Is Your Brain on Grief
This Is Your Brain on PTSD
Unfuck Your Consent
Unfuck Your Forgiveness
Unfuck Your Mental Health Paradigm
Unfuck Your Sleep
Unfuck Your Work
Vision Boarding
Woke Parenting #1–6 (with Bonnie Scott)

Other

Boundaries Conversation Deck
Stress Coping Skills Deck
How Do You Feel Today? (poster)